Margot Drink
July 2021

ATTACHMENT THEORY

THE ULTIMATE COMPLETE GUIDE TO ATTACHMENT: STYLES, TYPES, LOVE, AND PARENTING. INCLUDING A FOCUS ON ANXIETY IN RELATIONSHIP AND THE PSYCHOLOGY OF CHILDREN.

MATTHEW K. RUSSEL

Table Of Contents

Introduction

According to the Child and Adolescent Mental Health Association (ACAMH), attachment theory is widely used by doctors, lawyers, politicians, and teachers. As it helps to describe the relationship between motherhood and subsequent development, it is useful in several areas where it is necessary to anticipate and understand behavior. Although extremely helpful in understanding romantic relationships, it can be applied to friendships, family relationships, and even workplace behavior.

Think about it: If you understood why you were behaving the way you do, it could, for example, help you close your caregivers who were emotionally negligent or inconsistent in your upbringing. Once you understand the pain you have internalized and how it affects you, you can, with the techniques described, heal, and heal any relationship where your attachment style collapses.

As an adult, you fight with your partner every day because you believe he is the one who makes every effort in the relationship. He moved into his partner's apartment in a different city and even changed jobs in a new industry to do so. His dissatisfaction has increased, but he rationalizes his choices, saying that if he did not do these things, the relationship "would not work."

At work, you also feel anxious about the safety of your work when your boss criticizes your work. Although his boss just wants to move a project in a different direction, Parker takes it personally. With his friends, he is constantly worried about their attention to everything else. You are shocked, dissatisfied, and frustrated that you are not pursuing a career in something that interests you.

Now imagine that Parker understood why he decided to do and worry about all these things. It has, deeply, a restless style of attachment. He abandons his needs in order, as he realizes, to satisfy others to maintain them in his life. However, his growing dissatisfaction with his partner is poisoning their relationship. At work, you are not satisfied because you are in a field that you do not like, and you take criticism personally, regardless of your intention. With his friends, he cannot present himself authentically because of everything else on his plate, and that makes him very anxious because of the programs that run in his subconscious.

In each of these cases, Parker only needs to understand that a healthier version of his life lies in understanding why he is making these decisions and their real consequences. By understanding your attachment style, you will be able to commit and not sacrifice your relationship, you will understand the importance of genuinely monitoring your professional expectations, and you can remove some stress from your friends by understanding that a friend will not go. Far away.

Although all these changes are easier said than done, this surface-level example sheds light on how understanding attachment style really affects every area of your life.

Now that you have a good understanding of the broad application of attachment theory, we can also explore the ways in which it works in all professions, such as medicine, law, children's education, and public policy. Attachment theory can not only be applied to different relationships but can also be used to understand better the functionality of different scenarios at the macro level. For example, in children's education, understanding attachment theory allows teachers and caregivers to understand student interactions better.

Chapter 1:
Attachment Theory

The Origin

In pattern with the World Health Organization (WHO), J. Bowlby mentioned objective facts on the psychological well-being of destitute kids in the repercussions of the Second World War. He finishes up from this the capital significance of a requirement for a warm, close, and nonstop connection between the youngster and his mom figure. Her investigations feature a few mental ramifications for the kid survivor of maternal consideration insufficiencies, for example, an absence of scholarly focus, detachment to the next, or nonappearance of passionate reactivity. In 1946, as a team with Robertson, Bowlby explained his perceptions through research done on the results of partition from the maternal figure during the earliest stages on the later improvement of the youngster.

These creators saw that the little youngsters, denied of their mom and remaining in a clinic or a nursery, lived profound misery, which declined as the stay was delayed. All the more accurately, their clinical perceptions made it conceivable to feature three periods of noticeable and quick responses in youngsters between a half year and four years old when confronted with a division: the descent stage, which starts with flight and can keep going for a couple of hours to a little while. It is a period when the youngster shows profound trouble, and when he attempts to utilize his accessible assets to recapture his connection figure. The second stage that of misery reports lost any expectation of recovering one's maternal figure. The third stage is uncovered by a unit of the kid, where the last appears to reinvest the company. Be that as it may, when the mother restores, the kid does not show any conduct normal for connection as though mothering and human contact not, at this point, sounded good to him.

These perceptions, wellsprings of motivation for Bowlby, drove him to disprove the hypothesis of the help of the libidinal drive-by oral fulfillment created by Freud to reevaluate the idea of connection to the mother. D. Anzieu (1996) alludes to the 1958 article by J. Bowlby, the idea of the youngster binds to his mom, and talks about "a connection drive, autonomous of the oral drive and which would be a drive essential non-sexual." This hypothesis, accordingly, created because of worries about the weaknesses and lacks the baby who endured early partition and parental misfortune after the Second World War.

Created in 1958 by therapist and psychoanalyst John Bowlby and enlivened by crafted by Donald Winnicott, the hypothesis of connection investigates the establishments of connections between people. As per Bowlby, the social bases of every individual are produced and are dictated by the connections experienced in youth. For a small kid to encounter a fair social and enthusiastic turn of events, he should have the option to fabricate a connection relationship with at any rate one individual who deals with him, in a reliable and consistent way (what

Bowlby calls the "parental figure"). This obligation of connection is created over the term, accessibility, and nature of care.

It is by crying that the newborn child will show his demands, his needs, and his nerves. The connection figure can react to it and assuage it. Bowlby alludes, for the most part, to the mother, who is increasingly present in the principal snapshots of life; however, another grownup referent is conceivable. Newborn child and connection figures can, at that point, if the relationship is agreeable and quiet, immaculate their sobbing/reactions correspondence over the association, which will create developing prosperity. This connection figure will turn into a premise of security for the kid to which he can turn on the off chance that fundamental, which will, at that point, permit him to investigate the world.

The manner by which the connection figure reacts to the kid's solicitations (crying) will, along these lines, be conclusive for the youngster's clairvoyant and social improvement since it will control the advancement of connection examples of the kid fundamental for his future relationship. If the kid gets a positive reaction to his solicitations, it is on the grounds that he exists, and along these lines, it is significant. This individualization will permit him to advance and create positive family and social connections. By and large, the kid will get joined to grownups who will be touchy and minding with him/her.

During the 1960s and 1970s, formative clinician Mary Ainsworth built up Bowlby's hypothesis of connection by including the thought of "secure" or "shaky" connection. It is from her perceptions in the field that Mary Ainsworth will recognize various kinds of connections: secure connections, restless avoidant connections (uncertain), on edge conflicted or safe connections (unreliable), and scattered connections (shaky).). It is the nature of care received by the kid in his youth (reaction to crying) that will decide the kind of connection created by the youngster.

Working System of Attachment:

The fundamental goal of the inspirational connection framework portrayed by J. Bowlby is to set up physical closeness and solace with the connection figure. It is propelled by the model of control hypothesis, conceived in mechanics which characterizes direct as far as "set objectives to be accomplished, of procedures prompting these objectives and of signs enacting or repressing these procedures" (Op. Cit p192) instead of as far as pressure and decrease of strain, that Bowlby built up the idea of connection.

The connection framework that is set up in the youngster permits keeping up closeness with its connection figure and its interior product: the sentiment of security. It is just when the requirements of connections are met that the small kid can securely move away from his connection figure to investigate his general surroundings. This idea is creative and depends on an instinctual social hypothesis. Bowlby (1978) hypothesizes that "the obligation of the kid with its mom is the result of the movement of a specific number of social frameworks which have for a predictable outcome the closeness of the kid contrasted with its mom. This connection framework means to ensure and along these lines, the endurance of the person from a developmental viewpoint of adjustment.

In this sense, more than a hypothesis of the clairvoyant working of the individual, the hypothesis of connection speaks to an applied system depicting the social angles and the requirement for security. As per Bowlby, this obligation of connection, once disguised, would later fill in as a model for all the cozy and social connections of the subject. From a more connectionist viewpoint, Guedeney and Guedeney (2002) characterize this social and enthusiastic bond as being "passionate associations between individuals when they are in a close connection with others. Connection hypothesis can be viewed as a genuine relationship hypothesis where the disguise of the essential connection bond speaks to a model for all connections of the person.

Fantasies About Attachment

Above all else, the connection is indistinguishable from adoration. It is false.

Adoration and warmth are two distinct things. The connection is a sure state of a person's relationship and advancement. Love is a progressively intricate and full-grown structure to which the kid is not yet skilled.

The subsequent fantasy - the connection is associated with the should be with the youngster continually until he grows up (there are different alternatives: from being "appended" to the kid up to five, seven, ten years, and so forth.) This legend is additionally false. More absolutely, it is regularly misconstrued.

The steady openness, consideration, and care of a huge grownup are, maybe, significant for youngsters up to about a year. The catchphrase here is "consistent." According to Bowlby, oversaturation for a kid is additionally horrendous (and occasionally increasingly awful) than a shortage.

Mary Ainsworth verified that critical grownups (or grownups) assume the job of a dependable base for the kid, which he addresses in snapshots of dread, vulnerability, and torment. In some cases, to quiet down, it is sufficient for him to remain with his mom for a few minutes now and again more. Significant, so a critical grownup is accessible as of now (obviously, there are different conditions throughout everyday life, it is significant that each motivation of the kid does not transform into avoiding). Notwithstanding, youngsters do not require and even destructive to be appended to grownups each moment.

The third fantasy is mostly associated with the second, yet here connection is deciphered as something that detrimentally affects the advancement of the youngster and can hurt the improvement of his freedom and autonomy. A few guardians every which way bring and keep up autonomy up in their one-year-old youngsters, declining to answer a considerable lot of their needs, which such guardians decipher as "youth shortcomings" (for instance, holding a kid in their arms, assisting with something). It is important that such thoughts may bode well with regards to more established youngsters. Up to five or six years (and now and then more), kids should be soaked with consideration, care, love, they should be little. Autonomy and freedom are framed since the beginning, yet steadily and almost certain, effectively,

The Neurobiology of Human Connection

The human bonds experienced all through life are transformative. Therefore, they can possibly fix negative connections in the beginning times of life through later sound connections.

The connection is a trait of warm-blooded animals. In this way, the investigation of human connection neurobiology is likewise founded on creature investigation. As indicated by late research, the connection is by all accounts dependent on the obstruction of oxytocin and dopamine in the striatum.

What appears to be complete is that all through life, distinctive human connections share the neurobiology on which they are based. All in all, they are described by the synchronization of conduct and the reconciliation of cortical and subcortical systems.

Chapter 2:
Different Types of Attachment Styles

It all adds up when you look closely that how we connect with other adults is closely related to how we related to others as children. From the study of attachment, four unique attachment systems have been identified. The prime purpose of knowing these styles is to be able to categorize yourself and being conversant with your attachment style is the first step towards boosting your relationships with others.

There are three essentials, fundamental measurements that describe the different styles and designs of attachment. The first being closeness elaborates on the extent to which people allow themselves to be intimate and emotionally vulnerable with others by sensing a feeling of safety around them. Dependence/avoidance becomes the second measurement whereby it showcases the ability to accept relying upon others without a fuss, and some even tolerating the dependence of partners on them. The final style is anxiety, and it is where people are stressed over desertion and rejection from their lovers.

These styles have been labeled differently for adult relationships as it mirrors the contrast between psychological and emotional behavior of children and adults. The attachments styles in youngsters have been correlated to the following adult measures of attachment.

- •Secure attachment shown by infants- secure attachment in adults
- •Anxiety or indecisive attachment in infants – anxious or busy attachment shown by adults
- •Avoiding attachments shown by infants - both dismissive-avoiding and fearful-avoiding in adults
- •Disorganized attachment in infants - disorganized attachment in adults

Secure Attachment in Adults

This the most absolute form of attachment in terms that, if you have a secure adult attachment, being close to someone comes naturally to you. Others depending on you can never be an issue, and you also do not mind being subject to others occasionally. Such a person is not intimidated by the notion of being by yourself, plus he/she is not bothered about acknowledgment and being dismissed by others. In summary, both intimacy and individualism are appealing to these individuals.

Insecure Attachments by Adults

This style is quite chaotic. It is believed that they are in consequence of the attachment they formed a while back with their primary guardian.

People with insecure attachment tendencies are significantly different in the following ways:

- •Their discernment of proximity and emotional intimacy and how they handle it.

- •Capability to express their own behavior through needs and emotions and become attentive to by also comprehending the emotional needs of their lovers.
- •How, an individual reacts to misunderstandings.
- •Individual anticipations of how the partner is, and the anxiety of the relationship (internal working models)

The four adult attachment styles

The attachment styles have been formulated according to the measures designed for attachment, including anxiety, avoidance, and closeness — and the detailed descriptions of each as outlined below:

The Secure Attachment:

As described earlier, they are Low on both being anxious and avoidance. Very comfy and tolerant of the intimacy; imperceptible over dismissal or being engrossed with the relationship. They value the relationships he or she is in and able to express their affections verbally and behaviorally. They can freely love and receive love from others.

Avoidant

Fearful avoidant or Disorganized Attachment in Adults

Grownups who have fearful avoidance act in impulsive ways. They are very persistent in trying various ways to get what they think they need in a relationship, most of the time, seemingly not working. Their partners can hardly make clarity of what they are trying to imply, and neither can they. High on avoidance, low on anxiety. They seem awkward when it comes to being close with others and consequently values their personal space, unstressed over partner's presence being there or not. It involves people who are not keen on trusting and relying on others, and they incline towards others, not depending on them. According to Firestone 2013, the style makes it difficult to form and uphold deep, healthy bonds with others. Expectedly, this style makes it difficult to form and uphold deep, healthy bonds with others. This kind of person will often display disorganized thoughts and relationship patterns. Those with disorganized attachment style may have other causal diagnoses, such as Borderline Personality Disorder. These people may have had a devastating childhood of abuse, disregard, or recurrent experiences of loss.

Anxious

Anxiety-Preoccupied (or Anxiety-Resistant) Attachment:

Individuals under this category may feel desperate for love or fondness in that they form less secure bonds with their partners and feel that their lover must always solve their problems, promoting a feeling of completeness. They feel the need to be extremely emotionally attached to the others while the others are hesitating to get close to their liking. They are regularly stressing over whether their partners love and value them or the fear of abandonment. Even though they desire the wellbeing and hope that their relationships are secure, find themselves behaving in ways that ruin their relationships and distance the other party as opposed to welcoming them in. They ordinarily relive and recount narratives again and again of their past relationship mishaps. They may commonly review their internal discourse and remember most of their past torment and rejections, signifying an absence of goals.

Anxious and Avoidant

Dismissive-Avoidant (or Anxious-Avoidant) Attachment:

It is high in both avoidance and anxiety. Individuals here are not comfortable with being intimate or the worry of the partner's commitment and love. They stress over being hurt in case they get close to their partner. They do not see the necessity and would rather not bother with having a social environment to survive or flourish and demand just to keep to themselves without anyone interfering with them. This person may have earmarks of being standoffish and gets awkward when others endeavor to show love or a more profound connection in the relationship. They appear to be dismissive of the emotional and bodily preferences of the other person in the relationship. This individual will also have issues expressing his needs and desires to others as well.

illustration of the four attachment styles

These styles are not sufficient too to simply describe a specific sort of person, though they should be considered as a sort of continuum of attachment practices. An individual considered to have a generally secure attachment style may every now and then, showcase conduct that progressively fit in other connection styles, or rather a person with a dismissive-avoidance might develop a bond that is secure with their loved one. It is normality for adults to have a variety of traits as opposed to fitting into just one style.

Subsequently, these "types" ought to be viewed as an approach to depict and comprehend a person's conduct as opposed to a definite portrayal of an individuals' character. Considering a person's attachment style, the way the person at hand approaches intimacy in relationships or marriage, and even child-rearing can vary widely.

Herewith the four adult attachment styles are broken down considering; the cognitive, behavioral, and social sides of each style, with the manner in that they contrast each other concerning closeness, reliance, avoidance, and anxiety. It is a norm for grownups to have an intertwining variety of mannerisms as opposed to fitting into just one style.

Autonomous (Secure):

- •Agreeable with an amiable, affectionate, and emotionally close relationship.

- •Relies upon their lover and creates a space where the partner can also depend on them; is present for a partner during hardship; is consistent.

- •Acknowledges lover's call for space (individualism) without feeling dismissed or vulnerable; can be described as a dependent–independent (subordinate autonomous).

- •Makes decisions with a partner

- •Trusting, compassionate, accepting of differences, and pardoning.

- •Introduces friends and family at an early stage of the relationship.

- •Naturally conveys their emotions and needs in an honest and straightforward manner; receptive to partner's wants and responds appropriately; able to reach a compromise during a misunderstanding.

- •Manages emotions well, not over-resentful about relationship issues.

- •The understanding, resolution, and forgiving of past relationship issues and hurts.

- •Delicate, cordial, and attentive parents; sensitive to child's prompts and wants; children are securely attached.

Dismissive
(Avoidance):

- •Emotionally locked down and dismissing in a relationship's intimacy; brushes off the partner; partner always wanting more closeness; "disengage the attachment needs, feelings, and behaviors.

- •Losing independence and intimacy go hand in hand, value autonomy greatly.

- •Communication is intellectually versed, is unhappily conversing of emotions, always a peacemaker, then needs to get away or explode in case of a disagreement.

- •Calm, collected, apathetic, compulsively self-dependent; limited emotional responses; prefers to be alone.

- •Does not panic in a crisis; logical, assumes responsibility.

- •Emotionally challenged as a parent, unengaged and detached; youngsters are likely to have avoided the person as soon as possible.

- •Sends mixed signals; Doesn't make his/her intentions clear—leave you speculating as to his/her sentiments
- •Devalues you, use distancing mechanisms, both physical and emotional.
- •Has a ridiculous sentimental perspective on how a relationship ought to be, uncompromising rules
- •Doubtful feelings of trepidation being exploited by a partner.

Preoccupied (Anxiety):

- •Uncertain of intimacy in relationships; always stressed over being rejected and abandoned; engrossed with the relationship; "hyper activates" needs and behavior required or attached.
- •Needs assurance constantly; requires continuous consolation; would want to "merge" with a partner, which could drive a partner away.
- •Still lingers on the past, which barges into present discernments and relationships (with fear, hurt, outrage, and dismissal holding them back).
- •Few of them can go to the extent of manipulation and planning out actions to get what they want out of the relationship; likewise, show a solid sense of innovativeness and charming qualities.
- •Excessively delicate to partner's behavior, actions, and temperaments; is too conscious of the partner's behavior.

- •Exceptionally with high emotions; defensive in arguments, confrontational, very quick to anger and to control; does not know the meaning of personal boundaries.

- •Needs a ton of closeness in the relationship, Miserable when not in a relationship

- •Gives the partner a chance to establish the pace of the relationship not to get hurt

- •Suspicious partner may be unfaithful

- •Communication is not collaborative; ignorant of personal responsibilities in relationships; often blames others; Experiences serious difficulties not making things about himself/herself in the relationship.

- •Capricious and grouchy; associates well through clashing, "stir the pot."

- •Lacks consistent involvement with their children, who tend to be on edge.

Unresolved (Unorganized):

- •Unchanged mentality and feelings; terrified by memories of past events; not mourning or settling from losses from long ago.

- • In a relationship cannot tolerate getting emotionally close with the partner; pugnacious, tempered, unable to manage own emotions; sometimes abusive and dysfunctional relationships recreate perpetual past patterns.

- •Invasive and terrifying horrendous recollection and when triggered; disconnects to keep away from agony and pain; severe depression, PTSD.

- •Standoffish; absence of compassion and unapologetic; aggressive and punitive; narcissistic, rule breaker; substance abuse and culpability.

- •Prone to abusing their children puts their children into past unresolved connection issues, prompted into anger and fear by parent-child interaction leading to them being emotionally challenged; their offspring end up with disorganized attachment.

Chapter 3:
What Attachment Have You Got?

Directions:

This quiz is designed to determine your attachment style. In the statements below, highlight the answers that sound most like yourself. Refer to the key to find your primary attachment style, along with other attachment-style tendencies that exist within you.

1.

I can be very emotionally present with others, but it takes me a while to share vulnerable things about myself.

2.

I practice excellent self-care for both myself and my partner.

3.

I often put my partner on a pedestal.

4.

I easily feel irritated or impatient around my partner.

5.

I feel comfortable around my partner and enjoy their company.

6.

I have a strong desire for deep conversation in a romantic relationship.

7.

I feel terribly upset when others infringe on my need for space or time alone.

8.

I prefer not to spend much time alone.

9.

I do not make whimsical decisions about leaving a relationship.

10.

I tend quite frequently to be out of touch with my emotions.

11.

I am very attuned to my partner's needs and notice when there is any change in behavior.

12.

I express my emotions easily.

13.

I constantly want to be emotionally closer to my partner.

14.

I know how to process my emotions effectively when I feel upset.

15.

I easily notice a change in people's micro-expressions, body language, and tone of voice.

16.

I worry that my partner will fall out of love with me or eventually get bored with me.

17.

I am effective at compromising and communicating.

18.

I have extraordinarily strong emotions in relationships.

19.

I strongly dislike feeling vulnerable to others.

20.

If I notice my partner showing any signs of coldness, I panic and want to get closer as quickly as possible.

21.

I do not hold grudges easily or keep resentments long.

22.

I often express anger very strongly when I feel hurt, powerless, or betrayed.

23.

I do not feel as if boundaries are necessary between myself and a romantic partner.

24.

I feel as though conflict is resolvable and feel equipped to work through problems effectively.

25.

It is not uncommon for me to experience inward emotional turbulence throughout the duration of a romantic relationship.

26.

I can be cold and standoffish at times when I do not know others very well.

27.

I often feel extremely hot or very cold toward my partner or loved one.

28.

I know that I am worthy of a healthy, happy relationship.

29.

I usually wish that my partner would take care of their own emotions and needs and involve me less.

30.

When I feel hurt, I often have thoughts about leaving the relationship immediately.

31.

I do not feel as though I need anything from my romantic partner.

32.

I am good at listening to other people's needs and expressing my own.

33.

I often worry that my partner will reject me or pull away.

34.

I do not enjoy being out of relationships.

35.

If my partner's behavior hurts me, I will express my feelings and try to understand what caused them to act that way.

36.

Relationships are often confusing or emotionally difficult for me.

37.

I do not like making social plans with others in advance.

38.

I sometimes feel as though I am constantly chasing my partner's love and affection.

39.

I find it difficult to trust others in a romantic relationship and am often suspicious.

40.

I find that setting boundaries come naturally to me.

41.

There have been times when I have threatened to leave the relationship and then changed my mind.

42.

I often avoid conflict and feel very hurt by criticism.

43.

I am not afraid of commitment, but I do not jump into relationships without assessing them first.

44.

I am afraid that if I ask too much from my partner, they will leave me.

45.

I focus much more on the relationships in my life than I do on myself.

46.

I develop feelings easily but feel as if I am constantly doubting or questioning them as I get closer to my partner.

47.

Sometimes the idea of commitment in a romantic relationship makes me feel afraid or invaded.

48.

I often feel protective over my space, privacy, and belongings.

49.

I am emotionally stable in my romantic relationships.

50.

I tend to operate in extremes between being very emotionally available and then requiring time and space to myself.

51.

I find it too easy to open to people and sometimes overshare with others.

52.

I do not express my emotions to others easily.

53.

I do not tend to overshare, but I do not fear to share my feelings with a partner.

54.

I generally feel invaded when my partner demands too much physical affection.

55.

I hunger for closeness, but often fear to be truly vulnerable to my partner.

56.

I find it much easier to process my emotions on my own than with others.

57.

I would prefer to spend most of my free time with my partner.

58.

I feel that it is easy to express my needs to my romantic partner.

59.

I find that my partner usually emotionally recovers from the conflict before I do.

60.

I deeply fear being abandoned by my partner.

KEY

FA = Fearful-Avoidant

DA = Dismissive-Avoidant

S = Secure

A = Anxious

1) FA

2) S

3) A

4) DA

5) S

6) FA

7) DA

8) A

9) S

10) DA

11) FA

12) A

13) A

14) S

15) FA

16) A

17) S

18) FA

19) DA

20) A

21) S

22) FA

23) A

24) S

25) FA

26) DA

27) FA

28) S

29) DA

30) FA

31) DA

32) S

33) A

34) A

35) S

36) FA

37) DA

38) A

39) FA

40) S

41) FA

42) DA

43) S

44) A

45) A

46) FA

47) DA

48) DA

49) S

50) FA

51) A

52) DA

53) S

54) DA

55) FA

56) DA

57) A

58) S

59) DA

60) A

Add up your results in each category using the key above. Remember, we are not a single attachment style. Your answers will provide you with your primary attachment style, along with the tendencies you share with other attachment styles.

Fearful-Avoidant (FA): ___________________

Dismissive-Avoidant (DA): ___________________

Secure (S): ___________________

Anxious (A): ___________________

Once you have determined your results from the quiz above, it is recommended that you take a closer look at the initial core wounds and attachment patterns explained above.

As you come to understand the interactions more deeply between your attachment style and the styles of your loved ones, you will be empowered to communicate more effectively. You will also be able to understand what your sensitivities are in relationships and what is likely to trigger your loved ones. You will then be provided with tools and strategies that will allow you to break through the limitations that might exist because of conflicting attachment dynamics.

It is important to remember that your attachment style results are not a diagnosis. These are simply a set of patterns that you have developed over time because of your experiences. These patterns can be changed with intention, or they may change because of exposure to new experiences. Through awareness of these patterns of relating to others, you have a greater chance to thrive in your relationships.

Chapter 4:
Attachment: The Most Significant Source of Suffering

Without a doubt, the human species is one of the most delicate. At the point when a child is conceived, he needs his mom totally to have the option to endure. A lion's club, a fish, or even a reptile is more ready to become free soon. In us, attachment is significant.

It has been demonstrated that this need of others is not just situated to essential needs, for example, nourishment or warmth. There is likewise a profound enthusiastic need from the earliest starting point of our lives: babies who are not petted will, in general, become ill incredible.

As of now, from the hypothesis of attachment made by John Bowlby, we realize that connection is made from the primary snapshot of our introduction to the world with the two guardians and proceeds with the remainder of our lives. This is on the grounds that connection causes a reference to the enthusiastic bonds we to make with others for the duration of our lives, first with our folks, and afterward with our companions, accomplices, or our own kids.

The need we have for others is unquestionable. As an animal category, we need one another. We pale or bite the dust if there is no other individual close by. In any case, there is a major contrast between that instinctual bond that ensures our endurance and the hypochondriac conditions that we, in some cases, create in grownup life.

"Adversaries, for example, despise and attachment needs legs, arms, and different individuals, and have no fearlessness or expertise. How, at that point, have they figured out how to make me their slave?

- Shantideva-

The mazes of connection

As confusing as it might appear, we can just accomplish self-rule, if we can encounter total reliance. The system is straightforward: if during your youth, you have somebody who you can generally go to for assurance, you will build up a sentiment of trust towards the world and individuals. That will permit you to accomplish autonomy in your grownup life.

In some cases, she works and needs to leave her kid in a nursery or kindergarten from the beginning. On different events, she is so occupied with her own issues that she has no aura to be there completely and on the most fundamental level when her infant needs her. Or then again, it needs to deal with our siblings, regardless of whether we urgently required it only for ourselves.

It can likewise happen that she feels so on edge in her condition as a mother, that she topples the instabilities that torment her; at that point, it shields it from additional, as though the world were a steady danger.

In those cases, and comparable ones, we develop with a sentiment of full of feeling void. We become too much troubled each time we face a circumstance alone, or when we need to settle on a free choice.

In this manner, we attempt to discover an accomplice that gives us everything, without anticipating anything. We request unequivocal conveyance, and we feel profoundly baffled at any indication of a lack of concern or separation. We live because of a paranoid fear of losing those individuals who, we assume, will fix the deficiency we have inside.

From the Attachment to Self-Rule

Attachment to others is significant and important all through life. From birth to death, we will require others to ensure our physical and passionate wellbeing. It does not make any difference on the off chance that we are a fruitful Wall Street financial specialist or a housewife in Bolivia. We need others.

The issue shows up when that need is changed into uneasiness. At the point when we feel that on the off chance that they disregard us, we will be that little powerless once more. Who is deadened even with an undermining world?

To defeat this nervousness, a few people can utilize various techniques. One is the one we referenced in the past segment: search for a figure that bears that outlandish guarantee "I will consistently be there; I will never disregard you." Another chance is to settle on the inverse: maintain a strategic distance from no matter what making reliance attaches with others, so we never feel surrendered again.

We can likewise get dubious, dubious, and excessively requesting. We will ask individuals substantially more than they can give. What is more, we will everlastingly deny he blames, his inadequacies, his confinements. As though we were a little tyrant disappointed at not having the option to control others at our impulse

In each one of those cases, the enduring will be steady. We will endure keeping that promoter who "embraced" us, be it a couple, a chief, a companion, and so forth. We will experience the ill effects of the dejection of not having the option to build up private binds with others. We will endure by not having the option to esteem other people as they seem to be.

Steps to Dispense with Passionate Reliance

At the point when our joy is subject only to an individual, enduring is unavoidable. Crazy and over the top connection is the greatest trigger for distresses, blacklists, and loss of confidence. In this manner, we should be clear: it is important to dispose of enthusiastic reliance. A viable advance must be taken to be self-ruling and sincerely dissolvable ineffectual issues.

Enthusiastic reliance has a great deal to do with how an individual is thought little of or debased (case, for instance, of ladies' casualties of sex savagery). Similarly, we cannot disregard a practically obvious actuality. We have all done it at a given point. We mistake love for connection, and we are engaged with joins lacking correspondence. Indeed, even to the point of leaving our prosperity helpless before an outsider.

Allow us to learn, in this way, what inside advances or procedures we should incorporate to appreciate more beneficial connections. In which the enthusiastic reliance is not the guide.

1. Instructions to dispense with full of feeling reliance

A first perspective to consider is the accompanying: enthusiastic reliance stretches out past connections. It is likewise regularly obvious with other social connections: with companions, associates, family, and individuals in the earth. When all is said in done, it is a circumstance that can be reached out to practically any territory.

Frequently, it might take significant stretches of time until we understand. We talk about months and even numerous years. For what reason do we understand so late? Since that venture, we will, in general, have lost our passionate independence. We are dependent upon somebody to the point of not thinking or representing ourselves.

The instinct of this mental reality will, without a doubt, be the initial phase in taking out passionate reliance. We should think about the accompanying:

How are reliant individuals?

To survey whether we will in general set up reliance associations with others, we can take a gander at the accompanying attributes:

• happiness centers around one individual: not appreciate something besides being who adores and increases in value.

• Your bliss relies upon how others treat you.

• Avoid no matter what to take the inverse to keep away from conflicts.

• It puts the craving of others before theirs.

• He is possibly fine with himself when he sees that he is adored.

• Fear of losing that or those individuals who adore or acknowledge to such an extent.

• It effectively falls into passionate extortion.

• He wants to endure instead of leaving the individual with whom he has that relationship.

• Feelings of blame: if the other party does not feel upbeat or fulfilled, the reliant endure inconvenience and blame.

• He needs to have control of the other individual's life to be certain that he won't lose it: he turns into a sort of spy to follow even the discussions he has with others and quits carrying on with his life to follow that of the other.

• A clear propensity towards social disengagement shows up: that is, you just need to be with that individual.

• The relationship creates tension: the individual is forever discontent since he needs more and, most importantly, fears that they will leave him, which would be a calamity since he cannot envision existence without that individual.

Anybody might want to have somebody unique in our life. What separates a non-subordinate individual is that when they are distant from everyone else, they may have snapshots of despairing, yet that does not stop them to keep getting a charge out of different features of their life.

2. Make a rundown of things that hurt us and fulfill us

When the presence of the issue has been perceived, and there is a conviction of the need to take out enthusiastic reliance, we should make a subsequent stride. We will make a rundown of things that we have come to accomplish for somebody, and that somehow, have hurt us. We are not alluding to the activities we have accomplished for the other dependent on affection; however, in what we have done in any event, realizing that it was not what we needed, needed, or profited around then.

Remember that a needy individual does not concentrate on his own prosperity, however, on that of the other individual so as not to lose him.

On the off chance in which you need to change and dispose of passionate reliance in your life, the main thing you ought to do is consider yourself.

What things did the other individual have that harmed you? What have you accomplished for the other that harmed you? Have you disregarded fellowships, family, exercises, contemplates, self-awareness, and so on.? Have you been treated with the regard you merit?

In these situations, it is imperative to know about the enduring we have encountered. Everything left or consigned as an expense. Untouched went through is the nature of time on earth lost. How about we ponder it.

3. Reinforce confidence to wipe out passionate reliance

As we have seen, the primary factor of any enthusiastic reliance is low confidence. There are numerous alternatives to reinforce it. The inquiry is to give it the significance it merits and recoup that key mental ligament.

How about we see a few hints underneath:

• Start choosing for yourself.

• Remember your past accomplishments, your triumphs.

• Do not think about yourself, do not search for others' endorsements.

• Start new ventures, meet new individuals. Tests get energized.

• Work your emphatics. State "yes" without dread and "no" without blame.

• Take duty regarding your life and your joy.

• Know yourself, investigate your necessities, and wants.

• Heal your injuries.

4. Figure out how to be separated from everyone else

Life is prettier with adoration. However, it comes sound when we like ourselves. We cannot have a solid relationship on the off chance that we have not recently evolved as individuals. Along these lines, to take out passionate reliance, it is important to figure out how to be separated from everyone else. Have a good time. Get us under.

Chapter 5:
Attachment and Relationships

Numerous studies defend the influence of attachment in childhood in the subsequent establishment of love relationships. Depending on the series of attachment that has been experienced, there will be a greater or lesser tendency to achieve a healthy, toxic, obsessive, or distrustful partner.

Although there are many elements that can influence the consolidation of a relationship, there is a component that, according to studies, intervenes very clearly: attachment. There are different attachment styles, experienced during childhood, that can condition — never determine — the type of relationships we have. Therefore, several theories that discuss the relationship between attachment and couple relationships are presented below.

Before introducing the psychosocial theories of attachment and relationships, it is necessary to understand the role it has in human experience. Attachment does not exist by chance.

From evolutionary theory, it is argued that emotion is one of the main strategies to adapt to the environment. Emotions help us to survive, as they are alarm signals that the organism receives and that allow it to respond quickly and effectively to the demands of the environment. The same thing happens with attachment, which is defined as a kind of useful emotion to ensure the bond and help of adults towards the offspring.

Through attachment, a union or association is created between the adult and the newborn that is postulated as necessary, especially in situations of threat or danger. Therefore, from this theory, attachment is considered as an emotional system.

The Objective of Relationships: Survive

On the other hand, it has been studied that in the consolidation of romantic relationships, one tries to ensure not only their survival but also the continuation of their genotype. There are similar motivations in both relationships - between the adult and the offspring and in the couple - it does not seem far-fetched to think that attachment can also play a fundamental role in couple relationships.

On the other hand, parallels are found between the behaviors that occur in both types of relationships, such as:

· High activation levels in the first stages of the relationship.

· The security and happiness felt within the relationship - which is between adult and young but also in the couple.

· The fear of abandonment.

· Apathy reactions to the other member's separations.

Attachment Theory: Why There Are Types of Partners

From the theory of attachment, it is argued that during the first years of life, the child will gradually develop an interpersonal relationship model. This means that you will learn to relate to the beliefs or expectations you have about how others will respond to your care calls.

Depending on how those care calls in childhood have been answered, this is how the person will relate and establish different types of relationships.

Types of Attachment and Types of Relationships

There are three types of attachment, depending on the help, care, and understanding they provide. From this attachment, types of relationships will develop.

· Safe style, safe couple

The secure attachment is characterized in that the child can explore the world, but it feels safer when your caregiver or attachment figure is close. When you have needed it, you have been given such care.

People with a secure attachment style are more likely to develop relationships that identify feelings and emotions of worry and anxiety - in the couple and in oneself - and know how to respond to needs. They are people who seek others without fear or fear.

· Avoidant style does not rely on anyone

The avoidant attachment arises when the attachment figure for the child does not respond to their demands, practically never care. Therefore, and since they have not become accustomed to that, these children do not seek their caregivers when exploring the world; they do not seem to exist.

Relationships that arise because of an avoidant attachment are elusive. The signs of anxiety and fear of the couple are not attended to, and neither is their help sought when one feels that fear or needs care. Such care is not requested and does not seek social support to solve problems.

· Ambivalent, compulsive style

In ambivalent attachment, attachment figures sometimes provide care behaviors, and sometimes they do not. It is this insecurity that causes children not to want to explore the world since they do not know if when they ask for help, their demands will be answered or not.

This type of ambivalent attachment gives rise to people who, in relationships, do not know how to deal with their problems autonomously. In addition, they are people who direct their attention to anxiety and fear and compulsively seek that attention and help.

Attachment as A Predictor of Relationships

Attachment and relationships are not only linked to the establishment of the relationship itself. Some authors find the attachment as a predictor of a good or toxic relationship.

Hazan and Shaver (1992) understand that the pattern of security often leads to happy love relationships dotted with positive emotions and feelings of trust. The avoidance attachment would lead to an over-concern about ruptures and a very striking lack of trust. Finally, the ambivalent attachment would lead to exciting and painful experiences, much more intense but also more unstable.

Attachment and opinion about the couple

Other authors, Collins and Read, find that safe style results in people who trust others, much more emotionally expressive and who usually have a positive opinion of their partner.

Regarding those who develop an ambivalent attachment, they are usually people with low levels of self-confidence and assertiveness, with very obsessive love relationships and high levels of emotional dependence.

Experiments on Attachment: Does It Influence When It Comes to Relating?

Many and heterogeneous investigations focused on the analysis of the association between the style of attachment and relationships. Simpson, Rholes, and Nelligan (1992) studied the type of responses that a group of women had when they were supposed to go to an interview with a job. Those who reported a secure attachment during their childhood preferred to seek their partners' support to calm anxiety. Those with an evasive relationship used not to rely on their partners and control their distress on their own.

Similarly, in a study of a group's daily interactions, Tidwell, Reis, and Shaver (1996) found that people with an evasive attachment reported greater negative emotions, particularly with people who might raise their love interests. The association between unhealthy attachment and depression, isolation, and anxiety were explored after these inquiries.

Furthermore, Fraley and Shaver (1997) also found that the relationship is related to the type of behavior that the individual would experience before the couple is separated. Results were found quite close to those mentioned above.

Chapter 6:
Anxiety in Relationship

Attachment can be one of the most pleasurable encounters on earth. Yet, they may, in any case, be a rich ground for negative reasoning and feelings. Relationship tension may happen at pretty much every purpose of romance. For a few single individuals, in any event, looking at being seeing someone make pressure. When and when individuals begin dating, the beginning times will cause them limitless feelings of dread: "Will he/she genuinely like me? "Is this going to work out? "How awful is this? "Shockingly, such issues won't appear to die down in the last periods of a conjugal relationship. As things draw nearer between couples, tension can get much progressively extreme. Musings come flooding in like: "Would this be able to last?" "Do I truly like him/her?" "Would it be advisable for us to back off?" "Am I truly prepared for this sort of duty?" "Would he say he is/she is losing interest?"

You are absolutely stuffed with butterflies in your stomach as you step into another relationship. You need it to end up being admirably, so you are not positive whether you are making the best choice. Tension seeing someone is not unprecedented, so there are various individuals included. There is a great deal of stuff you ought to do to overcome nervousness seeing someone. Next, you must get a handle on the genuine reason for tension before you connect with it. Uneasiness can emerge out of dread. The dread of not getting anything right, and furthermore dread of not being the best individual to the individual you know. With a huge number of events, you are going to discover a person who truly treats you well. You may have the ideal foundation. However, you cannot get around to asking them. At the point when you proceed to your relationship, you will discover that you are anxious and terrified of what their reactions may be on the off chance that they really met you. At the point when you have done questionable things previously, the cognizant psyche has a method of reminding you to apologize, and significantly after you admit, you will be unable to dispose of your blame completely.

Uneasiness seeing someone can likewise be activated by people who have issues with confidence. On the off chance that you sense that you are not worth being cherished paying little heed to what you look like, you will experience the ill effects of turmoil. In some cases, there are constantly stressed over the future and frightened of the unforeseen. Whatever the clarification you have, uneasiness seeing someone must be settled by taking ownership of your feelings of dread. You must take ownership of your issues with the goal that you can rest and appreciate an upbeat relationship. At the point when you have an inclination that you are sufficiently bad to satisfy your accomplice, it is an ideal opportunity to burrow internal and understand the individual you are. We will be esteemed regardless of what we seem to like. You must investigate the excellence from the inside with the goal that you can encounter from outside. You should seek clinical help, and that way, you will be persuaded by figuring out how to esteem yourself once more. Note, that sort of dread will conceivably lose you a relationship.

If you have accomplished something humiliating previously, it is no big surprise you have such uneasiness in your relationship. For instance, a delightful little youngster has discovered a great man she began to look all starry eyed at, yet she has constantly been brimming with uneasiness. She would not have considered getting some information about the number of premature births she had had in her life. In case you are in a comparable position, it is an ideal opportunity to pardon yourself. At that point, making the subtleties clean will assist you with discharging the issue. Be that as it may, you are going to put your kinship in question. Your well-being is progressively significant, so coming clean will stay away from a fundamental sadness. You will even be stunned when the individual who cherishes you chooses to remain close by. Nervousness is going to prompt pressure, and despondency is the mother of pressure. Along these lines, tell the truth on the off chance that you need to make dependable connections; you are certain to drop a load from your shoulders.

Such a lot of considering our relationship will cause us to feel truly forlorn. It can lead us to have any kind of effect on ourselves and our companion. Best case scenario, our dread could even reason us to abandon love through and through. Becoming more acquainted with increasingly about the circumstances and end results of relationship trouble will assist us with recognizing unsafe contemplations and activities that can hurt our adoration life. How might we hold our nerves in charge and render ourselves open to somebody we love?

What Causes Relationship Anxiety?

Basically positioned, experiencing passionate feelings shocks us in an assortment of ways that we do not anticipate. The more we regard another person, the more we lose. In a few different ways, both cognizant and oblivious, we fear getting harmed. To some extent, we have a dread of closeness. Unexpectedly, this uneasiness likewise happens when we get exactly what we expect when we feel love like at no other time, or when we are seen in manners that are extraordinary.

At the point when we move into a relationship, it's not simply the things that are going on between our life partner that makes us on edge and us; it's simply the things we console about what's happening. "Powerful internal voice" is utilized to characterize the negative mentor that we have in our minds who censures us, fills us with misinformation, and powers our dread of closeness. One lets us know:

"You're excessively terrible/fat/exhausting to keep his/her advantage."

"You'll never meet anybody, so why even attempt?"

"You can't confide in him. He's searching for somebody better."

"She doesn't generally adore you. Get out before you get injured."

This imperative internal voice lets us change toward ourselves and the ones who are near us. It can cultivate the forceful, critical, and skeptical idea that brings down our confidence and prompts unsanitary degrees of doubt, protectiveness, jealousy, and nervousness. Basically, it furnishes us with a steady stream of contemplations that ruins our fulfillment and lets us consider our relationship, as opposed to simply adoring it.

At the point when we get in our brains, harping on such stressing sentiments, we get amazingly separated from the genuine connection with our accomplice. We can, in general, carry on in negative ways, to offer hostile comments, or to get juvenile or fatherly against our critical others. Envision, first, that your companion stays at work late one night. Sitting at home alone, the inward voice keeps asking you, "Where right? OK, trust her? She, for the most part, needs to remain isolated from you. She is truly going to stop you. She is not so much enamored with you. "Such emotions will increase in your mind until, when your accomplice shows up home, you feel confounded, disappointed, or dubious. You might be vexed or cold, which sets your accomplice off to feel disturbed and defensive. Quite soon, you have completely moved the elements between you. Rather than praising the time you have together, you may squander a night of feeling inaccessible and irate with one another. You have essentially pushed the hole you were initially scared of. The capable one behind this inevitable outcome is not simply the condition. It is the indispensable internal voice that distorted your idea, slanted your convictions, and in the end, drives you down a ruinous street.

With regard to all the things we are thinking inside connections, we are significantly more adaptable than we suspected. As a rule, we can live with the damages and dismissals that we detest to such an extent. We can feel inconvenience, and in the long run, recuperate. Nonetheless, our essential inward voice keeps on threatening the reality of the disaster. It might offer ascent to critical side effects of worry over conditions that do not happen and hazards that are not even discernible. Also, when genuine articles emerge, somebody parts ways with us or shows a fascination in another person; our imperative inward voice can tear us down in manners that we do not merit. It is going to control reality and debilitate our own capacity and strength absolutely. It is the cynical flatmate who, despite everything, offers misinformation. "This is all that you can't withstand. Just spot the gatekeeper up and never be available to another person. "The securities we're making, and the fundamental voices we're encountering are centered around our very own perceptions and adjustments. At the point when we feel uncertain or befuddled, a few of us appear to get getting a handle on and forceful in our demonstrations. In answer, we can feel possessive or prevailing towards our mate. On the other hand, every one of us can feel rapidly obtrusive in our relationship. We could pull back from our companions; separate ourselves from our sentiments of want. We may act by being focal, focal, or watched. These types of relationships may originate from our initial kinds of association. Our connection design is framed in our youth communications and will, in general, fill in as a working worldview for grown-up connections. It impacts how every one of us responds to our requirements and how we keep on satisfying them. Diverse connection types may add to various degrees of relationship uneasiness. You will peruse increasingly about your correspondence type and how it impacts your personal connection here.

What Thoughts Perpetuate Relationship Anxiety?

The genuine, significant internal voices that we have with respect to ourselves, our accomplice, and our connections are molded by early encounters that we have been presented to in our families or in the public arena on the loose. Sexual generalizations, just as perspectives that our amazing overseers hold against themselves as well as other people, will enter our perspective and shadow our current desires. Although developing inward pundit is unique, some regular internal basic voices include:

Basic Inner Voices about the Relationship

People are continually winding up being harmed.

Relationships are occasionally worked appropriately.

Voices about Your Partner

Men are excessively unfeeling, wasteful, and voracious.

Women are so sensitive, so defenseless, thus circuitous.

He is just keen on hanging with his mates.

To get so apprehensive about it. What is so unique about her?

Perhaps he has undermined you.

You cannot confide in her.

He cannot take care of business.

Voices about Yourself

You will never meet someone else that knows you.

Do not get excessively near her.

Chapter 7:
Living Attached Life

Why are you so breastfeeding? Babies should sleep in a cot, and you should not carry him so much, you will spoil him. Julia, 33, is saying, since the birth of her son was ten months ago, she is heard repeatedly. The metrics come from responsible parents and other self-appointed child education councils in their community, but their guidance is hugely unnecessary.

Since she often breastfeeds at the request of her baby, she often carries her baby and let him sleep in bed curled by her and even on her tummy from time to time. And she does all this because she does not doubt in her mind that the best thing for her baby and her children is to raise her baby according to his instincts and common sense.

And Julia's not alone. In reality, in most of the world mothers still raise their babies daily by reacting to their immediate needs, taking and wearing and sleeping with them and mainly as they live in less modernized communities without access to pushchairs, baby beds, or child-raising literature, so they do what is normal and keep attached to their infant just as our ancestors have done since the early days.

However, parents in our modernized world have a choice as to how to raise their children. With access to extensive information on children from the literature to professionals, they have done everything from sleeping babies to allowing them to "cry them out" because they have been advised to do so. It is no wonder that parents are sometimes confused about what to believe at the first time, in particular as many therapists and children's educators seem to be shifting their minds on the best way to raise children for each new decade and because some revolutionizing methods have later proved to be very popular and common for babies.

This is perhaps why we now see a new tendency to return to a more natural and "traditional" parenting "way of promoting close relationships between baby and mother. It is a way of child-raising that preserves faith in Mother Nature's know-how. In our contemporary society, this theory of no foolishness, which has worked well for mothers all the years, has been nominated as the "theory of attachment."

Throughout the 1960s, British psychiatrist and developmental psychologist John Bowlby (1907-1990) coined the term attachment when he suggested a theory based on biology theory between a mother and her child. Bowlby studied the link between mother and bottomed three, who was hospitalized, institutionalized, and otherwise separated from their mothers (Bowlby thought mothers were the primary attachment, but later studies confirmed children's connections to both parents). Bowlby first introduced his attachment theory in 1958, drawing heavily from ethological ideas, and he described three different phases of separation between children and found that, when separated from them, the more children connect themselves with their mothers, the less distressed they become.

Throughout his recent studies, Bowlby developed further the attachment theory together with fellow student Mary Ainsworth (1913-1999). Thanks to the "strange situation," a laboratory technique developed by Mary Ainsworth and her students for researching infant parents' attachment, they started to understand the individual differences in how children interpret accessibility systematically.

The strange situation was created in the laboratory in which the child was separated and reassembled, and the child's response was observed. Ainsworth categorized the different types of attachment into three main patterns: safe children who were upset when the mother left the room but easily comforted when she returned; anxiously resistant children who were extremely upset during separation but who were challenging to be soothed when she came back often show conflicts of behavior, who want to be comforted but also have difficulty.

Ainsworth found that these differences were linked during his or her first few years of life to an infant or parent experiences at home; a healthy child had encountered attachment figures that would fulfill his or her needs, while an anxiety-resistant or avoiding child had attachment figures that were either insensitive or incompatible with or merely inaccessible.

Bowlby and Ainsworth found that a child with an attachment figure that provides a safe foundation is energetic, curious, less withdrawn, laughing, and more social than an infant and that the lack of motherhood can contribute to adverse developmental effects.

Bowlby claimed that the attachment patterns formed in early childhood follow us all through our lives and affect our way of dealing with other people, with our romantic relationships.

Current attachment theory has developed from Bowlby and Ainsworth's work today. Some scholars disagree on how exactly the attachment theory would apply to an ideal child-rearing, but generally agree that the mother (or another attachment figure) should be present to protect the bond and be able to respond adequately to the child's needs. This cultivating relationship can be built by a parent, by babywearing (carrying a baby in the sling or baby carrier), prolonged sheep-feasting, co-sleeping, and otherwise constant attention and response to physical and emotional needs.

American pediatrician William Sears is one of the most influential and famous proponents of the attachment theory today. We have brought up eight attached children together with his aunt, Martha Sears, a registered nurse, and propose parental attachment by seven B's; birth bonding; faith in the sign of your baby's screaming; nursing; babywearing; baby bedding; alignment of baby body and boundaries; and baby trainers' attention.

In an easy-to-read style, Sears offers detailed advice on how to perform the kind of attachment parents that suits the individual family and lifestyle, with their extensive practical knowledge about baby development, and remind us that parental attachment services include fathers and can be performed by other caregivers.

And while working mothers are not ideal in the world of parenting, there are still plenty of ways a mother can practice child parenting and build a strong relationship between them. Sears suggests that the working mother responds and can meet her child's needs at home and provides a loving caregiver with the ability to practice attachment parenting instead. A baby needs to be held, borne, spoken to, but not always by the mother.

Many parents believe that an attached parenting style would lead to spoiled, demanding, clinging children. Still, comprehensive research has demonstrated this and found that attached children become more relaxed, independent, and friendly. Several research studies have also shown a clear connection between childcare and depression, drug use, violence, and later adulthood, even divorce, raising our children, raising oneself.

Like every theory, attachment theory has its adversaries, and most recent critics claim that demand feeding is responsible for the growing problem we face today of childhood obesity as it is encouraged by attachment parenting. However, this criticism was recently based on a multi-year study by researchers at Texas A&M University.

Department of Agriculture found a direct correlation between the time and quality spent by parents and the obesity rate of their babies and discovered that the longer a mother spends with her infant, the less likely a baby is to become obese. Conversely, the more time a dad spends with a child, the more likely it is that the child is overweight. The researcher and sociologist have expressed concern about understanding these outcomes and added that both mothers and fathers need to be directly involved in the education of their children and hands-on parents who set an excellent example of their behaviors for their children.

Other critics seem to confuse the parental attachment with "permitted parenting," an indulgent parenting style in which children and young people have the right to establish their limits. But attachment parenting is to appropriately respond to your child's needs, meaning to know when to say yes and when to say no. Parenthood attachment is a matter of relation and balance-not indulgence or allowability, but focus.

In the first three years of their life, Bowlby and Ainsworth's attachment theory is based on their study of child relations with their mothers. It is not meant to determine the education of older children and adolescents. Sears and other modern preachers of attachment theory, however, are consistent with Bowlby's concept of attachment as "a permanent emotional relationship between a child and a person of attachment."

Several different routes lead to Rome, and there are many ways to educate a safe, happy, and content child, and most importantly, to provide children with a caring, secure and stable environment–a focal point for all therapists–and provide our children with a good example.

Spirit Attachment Is a True Phenomenon

Spiritual attachment is like a parasite infestation that steals the nutrients of the physical body of its host—the attached spirit leaks on the host spirit's energy. If the attaching mind is of a lower order, it is argued that it feeds on the negative energy that emanates from remorse, manipulates, and leads the person to culpa. A spirit of attachment is like a hijacker and the concept of space. And on rare occasions, the weakening of its walls could be persuasive in the discussion of spiritual devotion. The attaching spiritual entity is also in possession of the total executive powers.

Overshadowing refers to the presence of a disembodied person. There is also a variant of this hypothesis that thrown away fragments of the life force-body attached to the living opinion are responsible for the possession of an entity and not for the departing-soul. It is known that such a condition can lead to eating disorders, mood swings, depression, and addictions in the spiritual attachment theory.

Two elements of the school of thought supporting the theory of spirit attachment are excellent. During their clinical practice, most psychiatrists encounter patients with distinctive altered states of consciousness, which matches the condition of possession mentioned during Medieval Literature, and some of these patients react to dispossession strategies and displace the suspected attached object.

No one can certainly say how common real cases of spiritual attachment are, and further work is needed in this challenging environment.

The concept of mental space helps us to understand the attachment of spirit. The physical body of an entity is within physical space, and his mind resides within a personal mental area— a higher dimension, like a satellite system inhabited by spirits or at least parts of the brain.

This definition is promoting particle physics now. The space in which mental events occur is different from the area in our everyday lives and the physical space defined by physicists. For example, the picture of a bear we can carry in our minds has spatial dimensions (in the absentia of a live bear), and we can place this bear in our minds at a distance from an imagining river and salmon in the river that the bear may appear to lunge. Nevertheless, we cannot intelligibly speak about the gap between an imaginary bear and its imagined surroundings. Still, we can do so about any entity that we encounter in physical space perceptually.

Mental space is very intimate, and perhaps electromagnetic shielding protects it from the intrusions of other people's thoughts. A believer in the above theory notes that mental space boundaries often fail and that we encounter unexplained telepathy and paranormal communications.

Chapter 8: Attachment in The Aging Couple

Attachment is just one of the couple's bonds, reactivated, especially at the time of the sensorially-dominated encounter. There is physical proximity, body to body, caresses as a reminder of the sensorially of infancy on which the first attachments were established. But one must always maintain the sexual and romantic connection within the couple which one cannot conceal even when, for example, one of the partners is hit by dementia.

Forage, it is the primary health and survival needs that can triumph over the sexual drive, even going so far as to make the spouse's affiliation with the primary maternal object manifest. We note a propensity in the demented spouse to assert the presence of the mother, for example, by calling his companion "padre" or "mom" to pursue it step by step (Godot syndrome), to present grasping behaviors... Dementia turns everyday life into something alien, unfamiliar. The patient directs his attachment behaviors towards the spouse as a charged figure to restore the feeling of security.

Yet, unlike the moment when the child is in symbiosis with his mother, even the most attentive husband will never do anything when it's necessary because he doesn't know the state of permanent regression that allows the mother to fulfill her child's needs in large measure. The spouse oscillates between moments where he understands the needs of the caregiver and moments when he does not understand them: "Clearly, everything that induces tenderness, happiness,

This propensity to care for a loved one was envisaged among "attachments" through research on the ontogeny of the caregiving system, with the idea that adult representations of their protective role are built starting from his own experiences with his attachment figures but also based on his new experiences with his baby. Specifically, the caregiving system involves the ability of the parent to distinguish his child's mental states and regulate the negative emotions that overflow the child.

Fonagy (2001) has shown in attachment the importance of representing complex internal states of itself and others in children thanks to the quality of the mother's responses to the child's emotional needs. What the author later calls "reflexive consciousness" would allow empathy to develop. Perceiving other people's emotions, distinguishing them from their own internal states brings into play the greater or lesser ability of the subject to separate, but this is a strong issue in the helpful relationship between the dependent older person and the caregiver, spouse or child, where it involves:

· To distinguish the caregiver's emotions in relation to a rational understanding of the circumstances, often unpredictable emotions of the loved one support (in Alzheimer's disease or related disorders) who no longer have the cognitive skills to understand the situation.

· Helping the person to distinguish himself from the other at a time in life where everything suggests that the boundary between himself and others falls (the "dream house" test mentioned above is A picture).

His role as an attachment figure for his partner, his motivation, and his commitment to caring for him depends on the style of personal attachment he has developed (secure) for the assisting spouse. Here we retain the hypothesis (which would have to be verified in future research) that the relationship history of attachment experienced during childhood between a subject and his parent influences the way in which he, as an adult, conceives the way to care for others (children, parents or spouses) and also the way in which he accepts (or does not) being cared for by the other-some people seek isolation

The elderly couple relies less and less on words and more and more on sensorimotor (holding), visual perception, contact, and physical support (in a sort of silent communication like that of the mother and her infant). A privileged and personal relationship causes many careers to want to preserve the exclusivity of care, sometimes at the risk of depriving themselves of outside support. Then you must understand how attachment is related to affecting, so that attachment and libido combine in tenderness. Faced with the "threat" of undue support from outside, the caregiver continues to be "the best placed to meet his spouse's needs" and tolerates any attempt at separation, even when the latter attempts to "relieve" him. Everyday helps generate weight. Like the umbilical cord with two-way blood circulation, this attachment.

The elderly couple's example also shows that the overinvestment of sensorimotor skills in nursing punctuates daily life and tends to isolate the couple in autistic functioning: the outside world then becomes inaccessible to both partners (the caregiver matures at the same time as the patient, to avoid "running away" for example). Indeed, despite the disease, the couple very often develops behaviors of "anti-separation," such as withdrawal from a symbiotic relationship to protect the intimacy and avoid intrusion or separation. The perception of ambiguity and strangeness, especially in relation to the needs of the other, sometimes this misunderstanding of identities (we do not understand that what was good for the other yesterday is no longer good today, the patient sometimes no longer recognizes his spouse as his spouse, so it becomes increasingly difficult to distinguish between Me and non-Me) makes each other a new par.

Therefore, it seems impossible to evaluate aid objectively in caregiver assistance programs, specially developed in recent years, when it is decontextualized from this intimate relationship. Own world of the couple stands out from the reality they all share. Therefore, the attachment must be regarded for each of the partners since what is commonly referred to as "dependence of an individual supported by his job" is, in reality, a relationship of interdependence in which each co-builds the connection.

Despite the Wrinkles, We Will Keep Looking at Each Other With Our Eyes.

Having wrinkled skin is not the end, not even a youth defeat: it is just a sign of a lifetime. If above all, we count on a soul mate during this journey, this voyage will be even more worthwhile. There are loves that, amid the flaws, keep looking at each other, because there are emotions that last forever, even if we do not believe them.

Relationship experts tell us that three key components underpin these non-perishing loves: loyalty, sexual desire, and healthy connection where there is a strong need for sharing of things, interactions, and a shared mission. All this makes it no matter how much time goes by, and we will always have that person by our side there.

Helen Fisher, in her book Why We Love: Romantic Love's Chemical Nature, says love is like a pie of chocolate. Understanding the ingredients is not enough; we must taste understanding if we want it or not. Above all, a relationship requires people to "throw" themselves into the void to start this project, and while statistics say that nearly 50 percent of cases may fail, sometimes love insists and is eternal...

When Wrinkles Surprise Us Still Feeling the Same Passion

For some, the image of a passionate old age, the image of an advanced maturity coming with the same youth love, may seem impossible. Nevertheless, there are many couples who come hand in hand at this point, and it is not by tradition or duty. Despite the wrinkles, difficulties, and routine, their hearts are still alive.

One thing we find interesting and discussed by various studies, such as the one published by Harvard Medical School, is that romantic love is often necessary for a couple to have a lasting relationship. Today this kind of love has some awfully specific characteristics and is even far away from the classical conception of pure love.

· In a lasting relationship, there is an emotional need to be together and to be loved. Through magnetic resonances, it can already be seen that the most stable and passionate couples exhibit greater activation of certain structures belonging to the earliest brain.

· Passionate love can move into a more relaxed phase in which complicity is reinforced. A stage in which there is always the pleasure of intimacy and attachment to each other based on respect and reciprocity.

· Couples who reach old age and wrinkles with the same affection believe in their love. But they believe in romantic love and practice it through small details, attention, and mutual care.

The Psychology of Loves That Last Over Time

We have all met some elderly couples who fill us with wonder and somehow allow us to trust that there are even those loves that endure in time. That is eternal, that is authentic…

The beauty is always gone, but love, like the good perfumes, is contained in the heart of those who continue to look at each other with youth and affection…

Psychology, anthropology, and science, in general, have always been interested in knowing which components build these types of relationships that are not only lasting but also happy. In 2012 the Stony Brook University of New York conducted an interesting survey that defined several key aspects that we reveal to you below.

The Secret of Couples Who Can Keep Love Alive Every Day

We already know that the three ingredients that feed the most satisfying relationships are commitment, sexual desire, and healthy or enriching attachment. Now, these three pillars add to a series of indispensable dynamics that further propitiate these dimensions.

· Happier couples always try to do new things together. One way to avoid falling into a routine is to allow yourself to experiment, learn from each other, provide new situations to further fuel the fire of passion.

· Respect your partner's independence and personal growth. That is, the most stable and happy relationships are those in which there is respect for personal space, and, in turn, it is possible and respectful that each one also has their hobbies, interests, and friendships.

· The passion for life is transmitted to the relationship itself. This idea would be no more than the eternal and healthy conception that one needs to be happy with oneself and passionate about one's own life so that one's own wellbeing will also benefit one's partner.

· A love relationship is a journey of continuous discovery, never a burden or an obligation. This is undoubtedly the philosopher's stone of every relationship. Understand that we will go through happy times but also through difficulties, and that it will all be worth it.

Being a couple is knowing how to be a team that is willing to take on challenges, to always go hand in hand with every dawn we have until the end. Because in the end, cowardice grows older than time, and the soul needs only courage and a good traveling companion to accompany us today and always.

Chapter 9:
The Psychology of Children

Kid brain research is identified with the individual and social improvement of children, and a child experiences a few stages before arriving at the grown-up world after formative speculations on the full brain science of kids. The brain research of kids has been concentrated from various edges, including inquiries of science and sustenance; regardless of whether the baby is a consequence of qualities and family or a result of culture and condition; just as different stages in the improvement of tactile resilience, comprehension, enthusiastic and learning through language and psychological advancement; mental and instructive development. The investigation of newborn child sexuality and sexual and moral development is likewise especially significant from a psychoanalytical perspective.

Kids are helpless and handily affected by every quick occasion. Things that are irrelevant or negligible to grown-ups just can leave profound scars or recollections in the psyche of a youngster. A youngster's brain is amazingly impressible and alterable, and certain exceptionally unimportant occasions can have extraordinary individual significance in a kid's life before the kid arrives at puberty. In this way, "puerile recollections" and "childish occasions" are essential elements for deciding examples of grown-up character. Some significant variables that can influence a kid's future turn of events and perhaps have long haul impacts are

1. Companion misfortune or addition

2. Essential body/physical feelings

3. Network split or parent separate

4. Residential maltreatment or offense

5. Sexual maltreatment or attack

6. Learning encounters at training or study

7. Individual occasions that evoked solid sentiments of dread, euphoria, distress, etc.

8. Mishaps or illnesses watched or experienced

9. Passing of family members, neighbors, or neighbors

10. Living arrangement change or migration

11. Companions, educators, or family

12. Enthusiastic connections.

13. Singular school achievement or disappointment

14. Movies, movies, books, or news occasions influence battling, fear-based oppression, war, besieging, and so on.

The components here are extremely normal, and each kid experiences certain quite certain occasions that influence the person in question actually, albeit certain general hypotheses are created in brain research through investigation, and the speculations have featured the association between progress or disappointment in their later life and youth eve. Lev Vygotsky is a portion of the principle of kids' advancement scholars. While Bowlby focused on the security between kids, Piaget focused on youngsters' psychological advancement across different stages, and Freud expounded broadly on a child's sexual development. Kohlberg considered youngster moral turn of events, while Vygotsky examined kid socialization through social contextualism. Every one of these speculations on different parts of kid advancement shows just the gigantic unpredictability and the changing number of variables that assume a job in kids' mental turn of events. The brain science of kids changes from social, physical, psychological, sexual, and moral. Here is a short record of every one of those hypotheses and a far-reaching examination of how these speculations can be utilized, along with the general factors mentioned in the investigation of youngsters' brain science.

The' connection hypothesis' was created by John Bowlby, a British specialist who focused on the significance of a mother or an essential profession in the lives of a youngster. In his exploration, he indicated that each kid ought to create and keep up a warm and personal connection with the mother and that any nurturing disregard may prompt difficult issues in the kid's emotional wellness sometime down the road. Bowlby's hypothesis is valid, and a mother should construct a solid physical and passionate closeness with the youngster at any rate until the kid is two years of age. Specialists around the globe have recommended breastfeeding, and the physical closeness between the kid and the mother is a significant component of this, which is essential once the kid has left the belly of the mother. The primary feeling is dread when the baby is discharged from the belly of the mother, and they proceeded with the physical closeness of the mother rouses a feeling of certainty and solace in the youngster. Stranded kids or youngsters isolated during childbirth from their moms require a substitute for themselves, or they may grow up as intellectually sick or burdened people.

We were given a total psychosexual hypothesis that underscores the sexual joy of kids, which huge numbers of us do not care to accept. Freud toppled the possibility of youth honesty and recommended that we appear with our unrepressed basic driving forces, slowly tempered by social adjustment. Freud asserts that there are various phases of psychosexual improvement characteristic in the longing that we are brought into the world with an accentuation on some erogenous zones of the body, starting with the vaginal, butt-centric, phallic, inactive, and genital levels. Through the psychosexual turn of events, the satisfaction of discovering conduct changes from the mouth as when you sucked and bit during can prepare and afterward at last to the private parts. In this way, the child gets total sexual satisfaction from the analysis by sucking, scratching, playing with the privates, and discharging poo squander. I do not really bolster Freud's hypotheses on youngsters' sexual delight, and the satisfaction in their physical sensations could be explained in an unexpected way, as I will address in another post.

The French-Swiss thinker Jean Piaget built up the hypothesis of youngster subjective turn of events, presenting four-phase advancement the sensor engine stage, the pre-operational stage, the solid phase of activity, and the proper phase of tasks. The main stage is the point at which the youngster creates spatial abilities and becomes more acquainted with the world through the faculties in the initial two years of life. The subsequent stage incorporates learning and utilizing thoughts as kids comprehend the importance of things, and it goes on until they are 7. The kid arrives at higher subjective development from 7-11 years through explicit authoritative stages and can sort, recognize items, and utilize thinking to take care of issues. The proper phase of action that begins around the age of 12 assists youngsters with understanding dynamic considerations, shrouded implications, and so on. Kohlberg introduced a hypothesis of youngsters' ethical improvement across six stages at the pre-regular, customary, and post-traditional stages. They incorporate revenge and personal circumstance and the need to adjust and work for social requests, just as the authorization of fundamental moral standards. In this way, good improvement seems to move from the confidence in' what's acceptable and what's up' and whether an inappropriate is rebuffed by all-around moral and satisfactory social conduct. Another conspicuous therapist Vygotsky underscored the significance of socialization and relational correspondence and the advancement of youngsters, as indicated by which social and social information is viewed as a disguise.

Obviously, every one of these speculations must be applied, and there will be a finished or full theory that gives knowledge into the psyche and activities of the newborn child that fuses every one of these hypotheses. Likewise, youth encounters and occasions featured in psychoanalytic hypotheses are critical, not just from a sexual point of view. The entirety of the general elements I referenced toward the start of this article ought to be viewed as variables that underlie youngsters' social, sexual, good, passionate, physical, and intellectual turn of events while learning encounters add to the subjective turn of events, the ensuing enthusiastic turn of events, and consciousness of individual passionate experience. Sexual maltreatment or different types of substantial youth sensations may influence the ensuing sexual turn of events, and separation or family separation may influence ethical quality. An individual who has been troubled as a youngster can either build up a dread of sexual activity or can show an expanding absence of sexual limitation as a grown-up.

A child who lived without a father can either be very untrustworthy or turn into a grown-up who has a solid feeling of parental obligation. Normal disasters affect kids, suffering youth injury through death or wounds of relatives or living in wartime may leave a changeless feeling of uncertainties or of a connection in the kid that endures into adulthood and even mature age or, then again, make a kid estranged, schizophrenic or disengaged in later life. In a solid youngster's life, it is vital not exclusively to depend on mental speculations for seeing how a kid creates and comprehends the world yet, in addition, to focus on the kids' occasions or encounters and apply them along with kids' hypotheses to comprehend their brain research completely.

Inside contemporary youngster brain research, occasions are fundamentally psychoanalytic, and particularly significant are the impacts of antagonistic occasions. By and by, all occasions, both positive and negative, ought to be thought of and used to help brain research, it is critical to comprehend the unique situation and recollections of the kid to level youngsters' "occasion-based" brain science with kids' "hypothesis based" brain science.

Connection Parenting Theories

"Connection child rearing" is an expression created by Dr. William Sears, who portrayed such a child-rearing strategy dependent on the central purposes of the connection hypothesis. By the connection hypothesis, there is a forceful enthusiastic association in youth between the kid and the mother, father, and watchman. The thought depends on individuals' desire to have associations with others, and it is believed that youngsters will profit by protected and consistent collaborations with their dads and moms, which will, at that point, catalyze empathic associations later on lives of more youthful individuals.

Over the most recent six decades, analysts, kid advancement experts, and cerebrum scientists have managed the speculations and techniques for connection child-rearing completely. Every one of their discoveries has highlighted one specific viewpoint: the mind of the child is' hard-wired,' and an exception should be supported.

Chapter 10:
Healing Pleasures

When you have spent most of your life caring for other people, looking after their needs, and pretty much-loving everyone but yourself, getting back to self-love is not always easy. Changing from an externally focused person to caring for your own needs is an essential part of your healing process.

The best way to focus inward is to spend some time alone. This will allow you to focus on meeting your own needs without worrying about other people. Whether this means taking a holiday or putting some distance between you and your daily life, do whatever it takes to get some time to reconnect with yourself.

If you have embarked on a new relationship, allow yourself to be loved. It may be strange having someone meet your needs for the first time, but you need to get used to what it means to be in a healthy and balanced relationship. Avoid falling back into old codependent patterns. Always be self-aware and look out for warning signs that you may be falling back to old patterns of behavior.

In your recovery process, do not forget to have fun. Making happy memories can help you get past your old hurts. New happy memories can replace the old sad ones and help you to emerge stronger and more secure in yourself. This is the time to rediscover your interests and develop new passions that will allow you to get to know yourself better and have fun as you do it.

When you rediscover what your goals, interests, and passions are. You can plan activities around these three areas that will help you in becoming the best possible version of yourself. Remember, your goal at this point is not just to ditch the old codependency tendencies but to create new healthy habits that will keep you occupied on the road to bettering your life.

One of the challenges you may face is learning to trust and love again. Once we have been through a damaging relationship, it is natural to want to protect ourselves by avoiding intimacy and relationships. Do not deny yourself a chance at happiness because you are afraid that history may repeat itself.

Spend as much time alone as you need to feel whole again, but do not give up on love and relationships. Ultimately, relationships make our lives much richer. Sharing your experiences with someone who loves and cares for you is a natural part of a healthy life. Always be open to the possibility of love and trust that you have moved on from codependency.

Overcoming the Fear of Intimacy

We have already looked at some of the fears that may predispose you to become codependent. These are fears like the fear of abandonment, the fear of rejection, and other insecurities. These unresolved issues make it difficult to open to others and form deep connections with them.

If you are on the road to recovery from codependency, it is possible that these fears will still plague you. This means that you must find a way to overcome them if you are to have truly open and meaningful connections with people. If you remain emotionally unavailable, your relationships will continue to be dysfunctional.

Emotional intimacy goes beyond the physical aspects of your relationships. It is possible to have a physical relationship with someone without being emotionally intimate with them. Emotional intimacy requires complete openness on an emotional level and the willingness to bare your innermost feelings to the other person.

This kind of intimacy breeds a sense of security and safety in knowing that you can be completely true to yourself without needing to suppress or camouflage your emotions. Getting to this point in a relationship is never easy, and it can be especially hard for codependents who have a history of dysfunction and abuse in their relationships.

So how do you get over your fear of intimacy? Is it possible to get past unresolved abandonment issues and trust people enough to let them into your life?

Here are some effective strategies that will help you get past your fear of intimacy.

1. Identify your triggers

In most cases, your fear of intimacy will be due to unresolved issues from your past. Self-analyzing and identifying what trigger your fear of intimacy will help you address it objectively. Were you neglected as a child? Did you have a bad relationship that made it difficult to trust other people?

Whatever your trigger is, it is important to realize that unresolved issues only leave you with emotional baggage that affects the health of your potential relationships. Whether it will take some therapy, self-forgiveness, or forgiving others to get past your fears, do not ignore your unresolved issues.

Identifying your triggers is the first step to releasing them. As difficult as it is, facing your unresolved issues is one of the best ways to unburden yourself. Take the first step to dumping your emotional baggage by seeking help for your unresolved issues.

2) Be your own best friend

This is as opposed to constantly criticizing and finding fault in yourself and your actions. The fear of intimacy can be enhanced by low self-esteem that makes you feel unworthy of love. This negative self-image makes you avoid getting emotionally involved to minimize the chance of rejection.

Stop criticizing yourself constantly. Focus on your strengths and accept your flaws. No one is perfect, and always talking yourself down does nothing but dent your confidence. Every day look in the mirror and find something you like about yourself.

Never allow negative thoughts to dominate your mind. You have the power to create a positive self-image, but this will only happen if you learn to be kind to yourself. The more self-confident you feel about yourself, the less the fear of rejection that you will experience. This will make it easier for you to open and take a chance on intimacy.

3. Find a way to de-stress

Stress tends to amplify our anxiety and minimize our self-confidence. Finding an effective way to manage negative emotions such as stress will help you develop a positive outlook.

Yoga, meditation, and exercise are simple ways to not only boost your confidence but also minimize the stress levels in your life. The happier you are, the more open you will be to intimacy.

Taking care of your body also helps to boost your confidence and self-esteem levels, which again makes a big difference in how you view intimacy.

4. Do you know what you want?

Sometimes our fear of intimacy has more to do with the person we are in a relationship with than with our unresolved issues. If you are not sure the person is right for you, then do not rush into intimacy. Intimacy makes any connection deeper and more meaningful, but it will only work if you are with the right person.

Figure out what you want out of the relationship. This will give you the confidence to either become intimate or hold off on it until you are sure of your motives and goals. Indecision can be just as damaging as making the wrong choice, so always make a point to identify what you want from a relationship early on.

5. Practice being vulnerable

Just as you cannot fish from the shore, you cannot overcome your fear of intimacy by avoiding relationships. Put yourself out there and take a chance that you can handle any outcome in your relationship. Start small by initiating contact with someone you like, even if it is just as a friend. The more you do this, the better you will get at letting yourself be vulnerable.

If you are not ready for an intimate relationship. Take small baby steps that will slowly help you get past your fear of intimacy. Start by opening to close friends and family and get used to being vulnerable and exposed. This way, when it is time for an intimate relationship, it will not be as daunting or scary.

Disrupting Self-Defeating Values

Self-defeating behavior is common not just in codependents but in other personality types as well. Self-defeating beliefs or values are a set of traits that reflect pervasive and inflexible traits that we have developed over time. Most of these self-defeating values are developed as self-defense or coping mechanisms to help us deal with our environment and various situations.

Self-defeating values impact your self-confidence and hinder your ability to have healthy relationships. They put you in a continuous cycle of repeating patterns that become the order of the day in your life. You start to realize that your life is unfolding in predictable patterns.

The danger of self-defeating values is that the box you into a little corner and minimize your options and opportunities. For instance, if one of your self-defeating beliefs is love addiction, then you will always operate based on a belief that your life only means something when you are in a relationship. This means you will be incapable of conceiving of happiness outside of a relationship.

Self-defeating values are akin to putting a straitjacket on yourself that limits your range of thoughts, emotions, and beliefs.

Here are some of the most common self-defeating values that may be impacting your life.

1. Perfectionism. This may seem like a noble idea, but since perfection is not possible, it only makes you feel bad about yourself. When you are constantly falling short of your unrealistic expectations, your self-esteem is shattered.

2. Achievement addiction is like perfectionism. If you have this belief, you have attached your sense of self-worth to achieving certain milestones such as career, income, looks, and so on. Again, this limits your ability to appreciate small victories in your life and sets you up for constant disappointment.

3. Approval addiction is another self-defeating value that predisposes you to codependency. If you have this belief, you get your validation from pleasing and getting acceptance from other people. This is likely to make you over function in other people's lives, which is a classic symptom of codependent tendencies.

4. Blaming. This self-defeating belief breeds the inability to accept responsibility for your own mistakes. In this case, you hold other people accountable for your happiness, your actions, and your mistakes if you have this belief, you may be manipulative and prone to narcissistic behavior.

5. Self-guilt. This is the opposite of blaming and is a common self-defeating belief in codependents. It allows them to take on other people's problems and take on roles like the enabler and the caretaker.

The problem with self-defeating beliefs is that they can impede our growth by narrowing down our thinking. Our thoughts ultimately become our reality, and your world will only stretch as far as your mind allows it to. If your life is bogged down by self-defeating values, you will find that your life is restricted to a few self-repeating patterns.

Unless you change your beliefs, it will be almost impossible to escape the destructive patterns in your life. You, therefore, first need to identify the limitations you have placed in your life with self-defeating beliefs and then actively start to change those beliefs.

Chapter 11: Methods of Resolving Attachment Issues

Technique 1

Contrasting Yourself with Common Attachment Styles

Characterize the connection.

The connection is the capacity of one being to shape passionate bonds with another. Exactly when a connection is in its most beneficial state, it prepares to build consistent and fun associations with loved ones. In any case, if for no good reason one builds up an uncertain connection because of a horrible experience, at that point, connection issues may create and make it difficult to shape and keep up stable connections.

Your ability to build up a solid connection style is not reliant on a one-time learned event. Or maybe, it is created and shaped again and again because of the various experiences and occasions that you are presented to at an opportune time in your life. For example, how the guardian reacts and sustains you as a youth, any injury you may have been presented to, and maybe a slanted natural, intellectual, or state of mind may influence your ability to create solid connection styles.

Comprehend the various sorts of connections.

There are different sorts of associations an individual may have. Truly Understanding the different sorts will empower you to appreciate yourself better, and if there are issues, one ought to be tended to with the assistance of a specialist.

People normally do not have just a single connection style yet give signs of a couple. By far, most of us have a mix of styles that regularly depend upon the relationship you are in and what is happening in your life right now. With that, you will consistently observe that you have a common kind with specific characteristics of the others.

Evaluate your degree of security in yourself and your connections.

People related to secure connection styles have high confidence and are happy with accepting and giving affection. They do not look unto others to discover approval. People with secure associations normally had consistent and cherishing childhoods. They had their necessities met and lived in a steady area.

Check for tenacious practices.

It involves being gruff with yourself. It is safe to say that you are tireless when in a relationship? Is it true that you are constantly worried about the assessment of others about you? People with this association style (on edge type) long for closeness and become fixated on the nuances of their relationship.

Those with on edge connection styles grew up dubious of what kind of treatment they would get from their people. Here and there, they were met with adoration and care, while on different events, they would encounter harshness and surrender. Along these lines, they are continually looking for approval and somebody to finish them.

Do you avoid closeness?

People with avoidant association styles are much of the time raised by watchmen who are coldhearted toward their kids' needs. They themselves are sincerely pulled back and regularly unsettle their kids from crying or showing feelings. They need their adolescents to wind up autonomous as quickly as time permits and have a little reaction when their kid is upset or requiring support.

Strategy 2

Surveying Your Personality

Do you such as yourself?

The way wherein gatekeepers treat their kids impacts their certainty for the rest of their lives. How you feel about yourself is a better than average marker of what association style you have. Be clear while evaluating yourself, and you will locate the most reliable arrangement.

Is it exact to state that you are content with yourself, or do you have opinions of self-hatred? Do you esteem yourself, or do you think you are futile? You are probably going to have a safe association style if you believe in yourself. Those with low certainty regularly have undesirable association styles.

How would you react to contentions?

How you participate in a contention says an incredible arrangement with respect to your connection style. It unfurls how you handle strife and furthermore reflects the way wherein you saw your people carried on in contentions.

Do you keep your cool in contentions, or do you leave and endeavor no matter what to evade the circumstance? Do you shout, lash out, verbally abusing, and guarantee to "dole out the retribution" during a battle? The reaction to these questions reveals your certainties.

Break down your sentimental connections.

How an individual carries on in a sentimental relationship is maybe the most legit piece of information when making sense of your connection style. The way where you react to your loved one and the way you associated with them talks an extraordinary volume. You must be clear with yourself in this division, anyway troublesome it tends to be, yet it is basic when attempting to decide your style. To find someone who suits your connection style, you should initially be familiar with your own. Consider the way wherein you react to the things your accomplice does.

On the off chance that your accomplice says that he/she will call at 10:00 am and the individual being referred to doesn't call until 10:30 am, do you take that half-hour worrying over what may have perhaps turned out badly? Or then again, you begin feeling feeble or begin thinking you have most likely been deserted? Be straightforward with yourself, and you have undoubtedly been known to sulk around or start contentions with your accomplice. Sounds recognizable? You are most likely a shaky restless sort that needs confirmation.

Consider how you really feel after you have invested a great deal of energy with your life partner. Do you, for the most part, need some alone time after? Or on the other hand, maybe you want to be in a drawn-out relationship means it will cause you to lose your character or freedom and becomes limiting. On the off chance that this seems like you, you could have an uncertain avoidant connection system.

Approach your hover for their suppositions.

It very well may be hard to survey your own character since you are so near the circumstance. Be that as it may, in the event that you ask your accomplice or your family or companions to offer their input on how you act in specific circumstances, you may get a clearer picture than attempting to decide it all alone.

Strategy 3

Thinking about Your Childhood

Get some information about your initial two years of life.

As we have now taken in, association styles are framed from the earliest stages. An individual's connection style is reliant on how he/she was dealt with as a baby. Question family members or any individual who was available about your parental figure during this time. Those answers can edify you concerning your connection style.

Ask people who were around you during this time how the parental figure responded to your necessities and if and on the off chance that they were predictable in doing as such. The sort of communication you got during those underlying two years preparing for your connection style.

Decide how your folks carried on towards you.

Recall how your people rewarded you. Inquire as to whether they were reliably accessible for you, sustaining you and accommodating you, or if they were pulled back or conflicting. The way they associated with you likely assumed a colossal job in your connection style.

Your conduct as an infant.

It is conceivable to discover your connection style by making requests about your conduct as a child. Ask from individuals who were old enough to review how you acted accordingly of partition from your folks. Their reaction can give you a comprehension of what connection type you are.

For example, ask on the off chance that you cried a great deal when your folks left and how your conduct was the point at which they returned. Did you quit crying when they returned, or did you drive them away? Did you at any point notice when they left and returned? Their answers can give your knowledge into your association style.

Search out proficient assistance.

Contingent upon what connection style you have, and the level of harm from your enthusiastic and social collaborations, it might be perfect for searching out for singular calling help from a specialist. If you are an adult who has never tended to any past issues with prior associations (even those as a little youngster), you may profit by viable helpful treatment.

Treatment will empower you to by, and large investigate your adolescence and life experiences as related to any disasters you may have had, or introduction to injury from misuse or disregard. Treatment may assist you with picking up the conclusion of past encounters, and create sound adapting aptitudes so you can improve your connection style to one that is progressively secure.

The effect connection mixes have.

There are three-three viewpoints for each connection mix; every one of them has various implications for a relationship.

Inspirational Outlook

If one of the included people has a connection made sure about the framework, along these lines, it implies that the relationship has a constructive likelihood. From the Attachment hypothesis, we reason that the individual with a protected connection estimation can approve their accomplice's information sources. They can go about as better emotionally supportive networks to their less secure accomplice in beating their frailties.

Testing Outlook

The on-edge + on edge blend represents an extraordinary test. People with this connection style read a lot into things and can distinguish the smallest change genuinely and conduct insightful. This astute capacity that has been joined with their tense weaknesses achieves finding to ends. To lay it out simply, two distinctive shaky on edge individuals are probably going to experience a relationship brimming with acting, jealousy, and steady contentions. The comparable is knowledgeable about the uncertain scattered + shaky complicated mix.

In the event that an avoidant singular matches up with another avoidant individual, there will be next to no correspondence, which may have all the earmarks of being fine at the beginning of the relationship as both have no desires from one another. With time the connection will likely get more fragile, and it is difficult to keep up the relationship.

Conclusion

There are some cases that need to be addressed through current and future attachment studies. For example, while some romantic relationships are true engagement relationships, others are not. Future researchers will need to find ways to assess better whether a relationship really satisfies the roles associated with attachment. Second, while it is clear why attachment behavior in childhood can play an important developmental role, it is unclear whether attachment plays an important developmental role in adults. We do not yet have a solid understanding of the specific factors that can change a person's attachment style. We will have to learn more about the factors that affect attachment stability and relative well-being to improve people's lives.

Humans are creatures of the trend, and due to an intuitive desire to recreate and correct mistakes from our past, we tend to pursue a similar type of partner and end up in a catastrophic cycle. Without healthy connections, we are forced to deal with mental health problems like depression. However, we are not obligated to continue bringing the same inevitable mistakes because our connection styles do not have a stone. (Abrams)

Attachment can be both positive and negative. As the Buddha says, the roots of pain are attachment. It is negative that one can place the destination of his happiness in the hands of another, which means that it is out of his control. This should never happen when it is raining in the sun. We must accept that no one is responsible for your happiness and love.

This misconception is why insecure people cling to other people, fear their flight, and put the burden on them to satisfy it.

If you can give love to others and objects, then it is possible to love yourself. Yes, you with all the flaws, all the tragedies you have gone through and all the mistakes you have made. However, I love it!

When you understand that love and joy come from within you and that no one else is responsible for it, you can continue to love others, but the terrifying and attached behavior gradually disappears. Then you understand that there is no case

Everyday life, not even the death of your loved one, can eliminate that condition of being you.

Like any other behavior change, when you know your trends and are happy to try to transform them, you will no doubt have healthier relationships. We may not change our styles in general, but we can understand how to make changes and not allow them to ruin our existing connections (Abrams).

The attachment principle implies a binary relationship. The two halves of the relationship complement each other. The tutor relates to the child and the child with the father. They all work together in most cases, to stay close and know what is healthy. If the father is removed, the baby follows, and the adult follows if the baby moves out of range.

Attachment depends on the existence of both members. Absence is as important as closeness. Improper care of a person can cause separation anxiety, separation, and a feeling of loss. The root of the bond is the trauma of separation and the absence of the most critical person in the child's life. The child's opinion of this loss confirms or rejects her perceptions in advance and may change her beliefs about the caregiver.

CPSIA information can be obtained
at www.ICGtesting.com
Printed in the USA
BVHW071051111120
593059BV00008B/695

9 781801 181112